CONNECT EVERY DAY

CHRONICLE BOOKS

SAN FRANCISCO

ISBN 978-1-4521-7270-5

Manufactured in China

MIX
Paper from
responsible sources
FSC™ C008047

Designed by Allison Weiner
Illustrations by Ilka Mészely

10 9 8 7 6 5 4 3 2 1

Chronicle books and gifts are available at special quantity
discounts to corporations, professional associations, literacy
programs, and other organizations. For details and discount
information, please contact our premiums department at
corporatesales@chroniclebooks.com or at 1-800-759-0190.

Chronicle Books LLC
680 Second Street
San Francisco, California 94107
www.chroniclebooks.com

This book could not have been created
without the thoughtful contributions of many
people. It's dedicated to the connections that
we create every day and enrich every
aspect of our lives.

INTRODUCTION

Find new ways to feel connected!

In the busy modern world, it can be so hard to find ways to make meaningful connections with friends, family, and even strangers. We're constantly surrounded by social media and digital representations of people living their lives, and in the real world it's easy to feel lonely and left out. But there are simple ways to reach out to others and create deeper relationships with the people around you.

The book in your hands is a collection of 365 simple ways to find those connections with others, whether it's reaching out to people you already know or people you've never met. Take the time to call an old friend. Send a text to a family member whom you haven't seen in a while. Say hi to your neighbor and ask how their day is going. Chat with the grocery store clerk and take the time to learn their name. Or simply wave at a stranger on your daily commute. There are connections, big and small, waiting to be made every day.

This journal is the beginning of a deeper relationship with the world around you and your guide to warmer smiles, more meaningful conversations, and more love and friendship in every aspect of your life. When you find a prompt that speaks to you, mark the page with the ribbon marker and commit to doing it sometime that day. At the end of the day, check off the prompt with the date you did it and write down any observations on what you did. Maybe repeat it the next day, or maybe move on to a new prompt. With every action, you'll feel more and more connected to the community of people around you, and hopefully to yourself as well.

SEND A POSTCARD

COMPLETED ON ....

REFLECT ....

....

....

WRITE A
LETTER TO
A FRIEND

COMPLETED ON ....

REFLECT ....

....

....

TUCK A NOTE INTO A BOOK

at the store

COMPLETED ON ....

REFLECT ....

....

....

CALL
YOUR MOM

COMPLETED ON ....

REFLECT ....

....

....

CHAT WITH YOUR NEIGHBORS

COMPLETED ON ....

REFLECT ....

....

....

SMILE AT PEOPLE ON A WALK

COMPLETED ON ....

REFLECT ....

....

....

STRIKE UP A
CONVERSATION

with the person in front of you in line

COMPLETED ON ....

REFLECT ....

....

....

CALL UP AN OLD FRIEND

SIT AT THE BAR

and start a conversation with
people around you

COMPLETED ON ....

REFLECT ....

....

....

JOIN A LOCAL CLUB

COMPLETED ON ....

REFLECT ....

....

....

ASK SOMEONE
IF THEY'RE OK

COMPLETED ON ....

REFLECT ....

....

....

LOOK
PEOPLE IN
THE EYES

when you talk

COMPLETED ON ....

REFLECT ....

....

....

GIVE SOMEONE A HUG

COMPLETED ON ....

REFLECT ....

....

....

INVITE YOUR
NEIGHBORS

over for dinner

COMPLETED ON ....

REFLECT ....

....

....

WRITE A
LOVE LETTER

COMPLETED ON ....

REFLECT ....

....

....

COMPLIMENT
A STRANGER

COMPLETED ON ....

REFLECT ....

....

....

OFFER
TO HELP

COMPLETED ON ....

REFLECT ....

....

....

SCHEDULE QUALITY TIME

with someone you love

COMPLETED ON ....

REFLECT ....

....

....

INVITE A FRIEND TO JOIN YOU

while running errands

COMPLETED ON ....

REFLECT ....

....

....

GIVE SOMEONE'S HAND A SQUEEZE

COMPLETED ON ....

REFLECT ....

....

....

VOLUNTEER AT A SOUP KITCHEN

COMPLETED ON ....

REFLECT ....

....

....

SAY
THANK
YOU

COMPLETED ON ....

REFLECT ....

....

....

ASK "HOW'S YOUR DAY?"

COMPLETED ON ....

REFLECT ....

....

....

START A
BOOK CLUB

COMPLETED ON ....

REFLECT ....

....

....

HAVE A
SKYPE DATE

COMPLETED ON ....

REFLECT ....

....

....

TEXT "I'M THINKING OF YOU"

COMPLETED ON ....

REFLECT ....

....

....

MAKE DINNER FOR A FRIEND

COMPLETED ON ....

REFLECT ....

....

....

HOLD THE
DOOR

for someone

COMPLETED ON ....

REFLECT ....

....

....

PICK UP SOMETHING

that a person dropped

COMPLETED ON ....

REFLECT ....

....

....

LET SOMEONE GO AHEAD IN LINE

COMPLETED ON ....

REFLECT ....

....

....

HIGH FIVE

COMPLETED ON ....

REFLECT ....

....

....

THANK YOUR BUS DRIVER OR BARISTA

COMPLETED ON ....

REFLECT ....

....

....

FIND A
PEN PAL

COMPLETED ON ....

REFLECT ....

....

....

GO TO A NEIGHBORHOOD EVENT

COMPLETED ON ....

REFLECT ....

....

....

SEND
A CARE
PACKAGE

COMPLETED ON ....

REFLECT ....

....

....

SIGN UP FOR A GIFT EXCHANGE

with a stranger

COMPLETED ON ....

REFLECT ....

....

....

CHOOSE
SNAIL MAIL
OVER EMAIL

COMPLETED ON ....

REFLECT ....

....

....

REMEMBER
A BIRTHDAY

and send a card

COMPLETED ON ....

REFLECT ....

....

....

BUY A
RANDOM
GIFT

COMPLETED ON ....

REFLECT ....

....

....

TALK IN PERSON

SIGN UP FOR A CLASS

COMPLETED ON ....

REFLECT ....

....

....

WRITE AN OP-ED FOR YOUR LOCAL PAPER

COMPLETED ON ....

REFLECT ....

....

....

REACH OUT TO A POTENTIAL FRIEND

COMPLETED ON ....

REFLECT ....

....

....

TAKE A WEEKEND VACATION

with a friend

COMPLETED ON ....

REFLECT ....

....

....

SIT ON A BENCH

and imagine the lives of people you see

COMPLETED ON ....

REFLECT ....

....

....

ASK
FOR HELP

COMPLETED ON ....

REFLECT ....

....

....

BE A
SHOULDER
TO CRY ON

COMPLETED ON ....

REFLECT ....

....

....

SEND A FRIEND YOUR FAVORITE SONG

and invite them to send one back

COMPLETED ON ....

REFLECT ....

....

....

BRING
A GIFT

COMPLETED ON ....

REFLECT ....

....

....

START A GROUP TEXT

with old friends

COMPLETED ON ....

REFLECT ....

....

....

LOAN OUT A MAGAZINE

and discuss the articles

COMPLETED ON ....

REFLECT ....

....

....

EAT LUNCH AWAY FROM YOUR DESK

COMPLETED ON ....

REFLECT ....

....

....

HAVE A PICNIC IN A BUSY PARK

COMPLETED ON ....

REFLECT ....

....

....

VISIT NEW PLACES

near your home

COMPLETED ON ....

REFLECT ....

....

....

ASK FOR DIRECTIONS

instead of looking at your phone

COMPLETED ON ....

REFLECT ....

....

....

SIGN UP FOR A ROAD OR BIKE RACE

COMPLETED ON ....

REFLECT ....

....

....

BUY TWO—

one to keep and one to give away

COMPLETED ON ....

REFLECT ....

....

....

GO FOR A WALK

at the same time every day, see who
else is out at that time each day

COMPLETED ON ....

REFLECT ....

....

....

READ
HOROSCOPES

for people in your office

COMPLETED ON ....

REFLECT ....

....

....

GO TO A NEW-TO-YOU EVENT

COMPLETED ON ....

REFLECT ....

....

....

SAY HI

COMPLETED ON ....

REFLECT ....

....

....

MAKE EYE CONTACT

COMPLETED ON ....

REFLECT ....

....

....

SIT WITH SOMEONE ELSE

COMPLETED ON ....

REFLECT ....

....

....

INTRODUCE YOURSELF TO A STRANGER

COMPLETED ON ....

REFLECT ....

....

....

WISH SOMEONE A GREAT DAY

COMPLETED ON ....

REFLECT ....

....

....

GO
BAREFOOT

COMPLETED ON ....

REFLECT ....

....

....

TALK ABOUT THE BIG STUFF

COMPLETED ON ....

REFLECT ....

....

....

SET UP A MONTHLY FAMILY DINNER—

whether with family by birth or by choice

COMPLETED ON ....

REFLECT ....

....

....

SAY WHAT YOU MEAN

COMPLETED ON ....

REFLECT ....

....

....

MAKE A
PHOTO
ALBUM

COMPLETED ON ....

REFLECT ....

....

....

CREATE A COLLAGE OF PEOPLE

who make you happy

COMPLETED ON ....

REFLECT ....

....

....

TAKE A BREAK FROM SOCIAL MEDIA—

substitute in-person moments instead

COMPLETED ON ....

REFLECT ....

....

....

SAY
"I'M SORRY"

COMPLETED ON ....

REFLECT ....

....

....

PRIORITIZE TIME FOR YOURSELF

COMPLETED ON ....

REFLECT ....

....

....

TEXT WITH A FRIEND

while watching the same TV show

COMPLETED ON ....

REFLECT ....

....

....

MAKE A LIST
OF PEOPLE

whom you want to see more and get in touch with them

COMPLETED ON ....

REFLECT ....

....

....

COMMIT

to a certain amount of time spent with others—

and without phones

COMPLETED ON ....

REFLECT ....

....

....

LISTEN

COMPLETED ON ....

REFLECT ....

....

....

EXPRESS YOUR FEELINGS

COMPLETED ON ....

REFLECT ....

....

....

SAY "I LOVE YOU"

COMPLETED ON ....

REFLECT ....

....

....

SHIFT YOUR PERSPECTIVE;

consider how the people around you are feeling

COMPLETED ON ....

REFLECT ....

....

....

LIVE IN THE PRESENT

COMPLETED ON ....

REFLECT ....

....

....

INVITE SOMEONE OUT FOR COFFEE

COMPLETED ON ....

REFLECT ....

....

....

TAKE A
WALK

with the intention of meeting people

COMPLETED ON ....

REFLECT ....

....

....

READ IN A CAFÉ

instead of alone at home

COMPLETED ON ....

REFLECT ....

....

....

EMBRACE
EMOTIONS

COMPLETED ON ....

REFLECT ....

....

....

EXTEND AN INVITATION

COMPLETED ON ....

REFLECT ....

....

....

ASK FOR A
SUGGESTION

COMPLETED ON ....

REFLECT ....

....

....

ASK
QUESTIONS

COMPLETED ON ....

REFLECT ....

....

....

SPEND TIME IN THE SUNSHINE

TAKE
CARE OF
YOURSELF

COMPLETED ON ....

REFLECT ....

....

....

BRIGHTEN SOMEONE'S DAY

COMPLETED ON ....

REFLECT ....

....

....

APPRECIATE BEAUTY AROUND YOU

COMPLETED ON ....

REFLECT ....

....

....

GO FOR
A HIKE

COMPLETED ON ....

REFLECT ....

....

....

SIT TOGETHER

COMPLETED ON ....

REFLECT ....

....

....

BE PATIENT

COMPLETED ON ....

REFLECT ....

....

....

MEET YOUR FRIENDS' FRIENDS

COMPLETED ON ....

REFLECT ....

....

....

WRITE A
FAN LETTER

COMPLETED ON ....

REFLECT ....

....

....

BE PLAYFUL

COMPLETED ON ....

REFLECT ....

....

....

FIND
EXCUSES

to strike up a conversation

MAKE
MEMORIES

COMPLETED ON ....

REFLECT ....

....

....

BE HONEST

COMPLETED ON ....

REFLECT ....

....

....

LAUGH
OVER INSIDE
JOKES

COMPLETED ON ....

REFLECT ....

....

....

TRY A NEW WORKOUT CLASS

COMPLETED ON ....

REFLECT ....

....

....

DROP BY
SPONTANEOUSLY

COMPLETED ON ....

REFLECT ....

....

....

MAKE A
MIX TAPE

COMPLETED ON ....

REFLECT ....

....

....

LEAVE A MYSTERIOUS NOTE

COMPLETED ON ....

REFLECT ....

....

....

WRITE SOMEONE A POEM

COMPLETED ON ....

REFLECT ....

....

....

OFFER TO DO SOMEONE'S HAIR

COMPLETED ON ....

REFLECT ....

....

....

CREATE A HOLIDAY CARD

and mail it out to friends and family

COMPLETED ON ....

REFLECT ....

....

....

SHARE YOUR SKILLS

COMPLETED ON ....

REFLECT ....

....

....

SEND AN ANIMATED GIF

for no reason at all

COMPLETED ON ....

REFLECT ....

....

....

THROW
A PARTY

COMPLETED ON ....

REFLECT ....

....

....

PLAY
BOARD
GAMES

COMPLETED ON ....

REFLECT ....

....

....

PLAY OUTSIDE

COMPLETED ON ....

REFLECT ....

....

....

TRUTH OR DARE—

it's not just for high school

TAKE A SPONTANEOUS DAY TRIP

COMPLETED ON ....

REFLECT ....

....

....

TRADE FAVORITE PODCASTS

with someone you meet

ENJOY YOUR OWN COMPANY

COMPLETED ON ....

REFLECT ....

....

....

JOIN A COMMUNITY GARDEN

COMPLETED ON ....

REFLECT ....

....

....

ASK FOR ADVICE

COMPLETED ON ....

REFLECT ....

....

....

HOST A
MOVIE NIGHT

COMPLETED ON ....

REFLECT ....

....

....

KISS
GOODBYE

COMPLETED ON ....

REFLECT ....

....

....

FIST
BUMP

LEARN THE NAME OF YOUR MAIL CARRIER

COMPLETED ON ....

REFLECT ....

....

....

TRUST
OTHERS

COMPLETED ON ....

REFLECT ....

....

....

SEND A THANK-YOU NOTE

COMPLETED ON ....

REFLECT ....

....

....

SAY "BLESS YOU"

when you hear someone sneeze

COMPLETED ON ....

REFLECT ....

....

....

KEEP YOUR PHONE IN YOUR POCKET

COMPLETED ON ....

REFLECT ....

....

....

SKIP THE HEADPHONES

and listen to what's around instead

COMPLETED ON ....

REFLECT ....

....

....

SIT ON THE FRONT STEPS

COMPLETED ON ....

REFLECT ....

....

....

SLOW
DOWN

COMPLETED ON ....

REFLECT ....

....

....

EMAIL AN ARTICLE TO A FRIEND

COMPLETED ON ....

REFLECT ....

....

....

SHARE THE SECOND COOKIE

PLAY A GAME

COMPLETED ON ....

REFLECT ....

....

....

BAKE A TREAT TO SHARE

COMPLETED ON ....

REFLECT ....

....

....

BROWSE A STORE

and ask the clerk for recommendations

COMPLETED ON ....

REFLECT ....

....

....

HAVE A
SLEEPOVER

COMPLETED ON ....

REFLECT ....

....

....

REACH OUT TO A FORMER COWORKER

COMPLETED ON ....

REFLECT ....

....

....

TAKE THE LONG WAY HOME

and see what's new to you

COMPLETED ON ....

REFLECT ....

....

....

SAY YES

COMPLETED ON ....

REFLECT ....

....

....

TELL A JOKE

COMPLETED ON ....

REFLECT ....

....

....

WATCH A
SPORTS GAME
IN A BAR

COMPLETED ON ....

REFLECT ....

....

....

INVITE PEOPLE OVER FOR A TV EVENT

COMPLETED ON ....

REFLECT ....

....

....

WAVE AT SOMEONE YOU DON'T KNOW

COMPLETED ON ....

REFLECT ....

....

....

DONATE TO A GOOD CAUSE

COMPLETED ON ....

REFLECT ....

....

....

READ ABOUT PEOPLE

whose lives are different from yours

COMPLETED ON ....

REFLECT ....

....

....

PRACTICE
EMPATHY

# BE OPEN-MINDED

COMPLETED ON ....

REFLECT ....

....

....

TALK ABOUT DIFFERENT BELIEFS

COMPLETED ON ....

REFLECT ....

....

....

LEARN ABOUT A CULTURE

that you're not familiar with

COMPLETED ON ....

REFLECT ....

....

....

PRACTICE
GRATITUDE

COMPLETED ON ....

REFLECT ....

....

....

TEXT A
FRIEND

whom you haven't seen in a while

COMPLETED ON ....

REFLECT ....

....

....

SAY HI TO EVERYONE YOU PASS

on your morning commute

COMPLETED ON ....

REFLECT ....

....

....

MAKE TIME FOR A FAMILY MEMBER

you haven't seen in a while

COMPLETED ON ....

REFLECT ....

....

....

GET COFFEE WITH A COWORKER

COMPLETED ON ....

REFLECT ....

....

....

DONATE YOUR TIME TO A LOCAL SCHOOL

COMPLETED ON ....

REFLECT ....

....

....

BRING
FOOD TO
A FRIEND

who needs some comfort

COMPLETED ON ....

REFLECT ....

....

....

BUY FLOWERS
FOR SOMEONE
YOU LOVE

COMPLETED ON ....

REFLECT ....

....

....

TAKE THE TIME TO TALK

about your day with someone

COMPLETED ON ....

REFLECT ....

....

....

TEXT
YOUR DAD

COMPLETED ON ....

REFLECT ....

....

....

BREAK THE
ICE IN THE
ELEVATOR

COMPLETED ON ....

REFLECT ....

....

....

PET A DOG
(ASK THEIR
OWNER FIRST)

COMPLETED ON ....

REFLECT ....

....

....

OFFER TO BABYSIT

COMPLETED ON ....

REFLECT ....

....

....

MAKE A HANDMADE CARD

COMPLETED ON ....

REFLECT ....

....

....

GIVE UP YOUR SEAT

for someone on the bus

COMPLETED ON ....

REFLECT ....

....

....

PAY FOR THE PERSON BEHIND YOU IN LINE

COMPLETED ON ....

REFLECT ....

....

....

GO TO A LIVE SHOW

COMPLETED ON ....

REFLECT ....

....

....

TRY AN OPEN MIC NIGHT

COMPLETED ON ....

REFLECT ....

....

....

SEE A LOCAL COMEDY SHOW

COMPLETED ON ....

REFLECT ....

....

....

SAY HELLO
TO SOMEONE YOU
SEE EVERY DAY

but have never spoken with

COMPLETED ON ....

REFLECT ....

....

....

ASK A NEW COWORKER TO LUNCH

COMPLETED ON ....

REFLECT ....

....

....

SHARE YOUR BOOKS

COMPLETED ON ....

REFLECT ....

....

....

INTRODUCE YOURSELF

to the person seated next to you

COMPLETED ON ....

REFLECT ....

....

....

ASK YOUR SIBLINGS

about their new favorite TV shows

COMPLETED ON ....

REFLECT ....

....

....

PRINT OUT PHOTOS

and send them to people in the mail

COMPLETED ON ....

REFLECT ....

....

....

PASS A NOTE TO A FRIEND

COMPLETED ON ....

REFLECT ....

....

....

EAT
TOGETHER

COMPLETED ON ....

REFLECT ....

....

....

BE CURIOUS

COMPLETED ON ....

REFLECT ....

....

....

READ TOGETHER

COMPLETED ON ....

REFLECT ....

....

....

ASK ABOUT SOMEONE'S INTERESTS

COMPLETED ON ....

REFLECT ....

....

....

GREET PEOPLE WITH A SMILE

COMPLETED ON ....

REFLECT ....

....

....

SHOW UP AT A FRIEND'S HOUSE TO SAY HI

COMPLETED ON ....

REFLECT ....

....

....

PUT EXTRA MONEY IN THE METER

COMPLETED ON ....

REFLECT ....

....

....

HOLD
HANDS

COMPLETED ON ....

REFLECT ....

....

....

PAT SOMEONE ON THE BACK

COMPLETED ON ....

REFLECT ....

....

....

SHARE THINGS ABOUT YOURSELF

COMPLETED ON ....

REFLECT ....

....

....

KARAOKE

COMPLETED ON ....

REFLECT ....

....

....

COOK TOGETHER

COMPLETED ON ....

REFLECT ....

....

....

GO TO A
MUSEUM

and watch people watching the art

COMPLETED ON ....

REFLECT ....

....

....

HOST A BAKE SALE

and give the money to charity

COMPLETED ON ....

REFLECT ....

....

....

DONATE BLOOD

TUTOR STUDENTS IN YOUR AREA

COMPLETED ON ....

REFLECT ....

....

....

RESEARCH
YOUR
ANCESTRY

COMPLETED ON ....

REFLECT ....

....

....

ASK YOUR OLDEST RELATIVE

about your family

COMPLETED ON ....

REFLECT ....

....

....

REVIVE A
FAMILY
TRADITION

COMPLETED ON ....

REFLECT ....

....

....

ORGANIZE
A FAMILY
REUNION

COMPLETED ON ....

REFLECT ....

....

....

INTRODUCE YOURSELF FIRST

COMPLETED ON ....

REFLECT ....

....

....

MEET
SOMEONE
NEW

COMPLETED ON ....

REFLECT ....

....

....

MAKE A SECRET HANDSHAKE

COMPLETED ON ....

REFLECT ....

....

....

SWEEP OR SHOVEL THE STEPS

for a neighbor

COMPLETED ON ....

REFLECT ....

....

....

HELP SOMEONE CARRY THEIR GROCERIES

COMPLETED ON ....

REFLECT ....

....

....

TALK ABOUT A SHARED EXPERIENCE

COMPLETED ON ....

REFLECT ....

....

....

REMINISCE WITH OLD FRIENDS

MAKE PLANS TO HANG OUT

with a friend

COMPLETED ON ....

REFLECT ....

....

....

TAKE THE FIRST STEP

in reaching out to someone

COMPLETED ON ....

REFLECT ....

....

....

ASK SOMEONE FOR THE WI-FI PASSWORD

COMPLETED ON ....

REFLECT ....

....

....

LOOK ONLINE FOR PEOPLE

who share your interests

COMPLETED ON ....

REFLECT ....

....

....

GO TO A LOCAL GOVERNMENT PUBLIC MEETING

COMPLETED ON ....

REFLECT ....

....

....

SHOW YOUR APPRECIATION

to the people around you

COMPLETED ON ....

REFLECT ....

....

....

RAISE A TOAST

COMPLETED ON ....

REFLECT ....

....

....

READ OUT LOUD TO SOMEONE

LEAVE A COMMENT

COMPLETED ON ....

REFLECT ....

....

....

SHARE BIG NEWS IN PERSON

COMPLETED ON ....

REFLECT ....

....

....

MAIL ANNOUNCEMENTS FOR BIG EVENTS

COMPLETED ON ....

REFLECT ....

....

....

TELL SOMEONE THEIR BABY IS CUTE

COMPLETED ON ....

REFLECT ....

....

....

PLAN A TRIP TOGETHER

COMPLETED ON ....

REFLECT ....

....

....

GO TO A BLOCK PARTY

COMPLETED ON ....

REFLECT ....

....

....

GIVE HANDMADE GIFTS

to your neighbors

COMPLETED ON ....

REFLECT ....

....

....

HAVE A
POTLUCK

COMPLETED ON ....

REFLECT ....

....

....

TEACH
A SKILL

COMPLETED ON ....

REFLECT ....

....

....

STEP OUT
OF YOUR
COMFORT ZONE

COMPLETED ON ....

REFLECT ....

....

....

BECOME A
REGULAR

COMPLETED ON ....

REFLECT ....

....

....

TELL SOMEONE THEIR DOG IS ADORABLE

COMPLETED ON ....

REFLECT ....

....

....

SEND
PAPER
INVITATIONS

COMPLETED ON ....

REFLECT ....

....

....

GREET NEW NEIGHBORS

when they move in

COMPLETED ON ....

REFLECT ....

....

....

HANG OUT IN POPULAR SPOTS

COMPLETED ON ....

REFLECT ....

....

....

BOND OVER LITTLE THINGS

FIND AN EXERCISE BUDDY

COMPLETED ON ....

REFLECT ....

....

....

GO OUT FOR BRUNCH

with your oldest friend

COMPLETED ON ....

REFLECT ....

....

....

WRITE YOUR NEWEST FRIEND A NOTE

COMPLETED ON ....

REFLECT ....

....

....

SPEND TIME

with your youngest cousin,
niece, or nephew

COMPLETED ON ....

REFLECT ....

....

....

USE SHOPPING AS AN EXCUSE

to people watch

COMPLETED ON ....

REFLECT ....

....

....

PUT CANDY OUT ON YOUR DESK

COMPLETED ON ....

REFLECT ....

....

....

EXPLORE TRAILS NEAR YOU

COMPLETED ON ....

REFLECT ....

....

....

BREAK YOUR SNACK IN HALF

and share it

COMPLETED ON ....

REFLECT ....

....

....

TEXT A JOKE TO A FRIEND

COMPLETED ON ....

REFLECT ....

....

....

TAKE A DANCE LESSON

COMPLETED ON ....

REFLECT ....

....

....

SIT DOWN WITH SOME-ONE NEW

COMPLETED ON ....

REFLECT ....

....

....

ORGANIZE A POKER NIGHT

COMPLETED ON ....

REFLECT ....

....

....

JOIN A PICKUP GAME OF BASKETBALL

or some other sport

COMPLETED ON ....

REFLECT ....

....

....

CHECK OUT YARD SALES

and chat with the sellers

COMPLETED ON ....

REFLECT ....

....

....

BIKE AROUND YOUR NEIGHBORHOOD

COMPLETED ON ....

REFLECT ....

....

....

BRING TREATS BACK FROM A TRIP

COMPLETED ON ....

REFLECT ....

....

....

SWAP
FAVORITE
MOVIES

with a new friend

COMPLETED ON ....

REFLECT ....

....

....

SIGN UP FOR A WALKING TOUR

in your area

COMPLETED ON ....

REFLECT ....

....

....

GO TO A FREE DAY AT A LOCAL MUSEUM

COMPLETED ON ....

REFLECT ....

....

....

JOIN A FANTASY SPORTS LEAGUE

FIND A
LOCAL LECTURE
TO ATTEND

COMPLETED ON ....

REFLECT ....

....

....

PARTICIPATE IN A NEIGHBOR-HOOD CLEANUP

COMPLETED ON ....

REFLECT ....

....

....

RECOMMEND A BOOK TO SOMEONE

COMPLETED ON ....

REFLECT ....

....

....

GET INVOLVED

with your local public access station

WRITE A LETTER

to your future self

COMPLETED ON ....

REFLECT ....

....

....

READ YOUR LOCAL PAPER

COMPLETED ON ....

REFLECT ....

....

....

VOLUNTEER

for a local political campaign

COMPLETED ON ....

REFLECT ....

....

....

HOST A CLOTHING SWAP

COMPLETED ON ....

REFLECT ....

....

....

PLAY FRISBEE AT THE PARK

COMPLETED ON ....

REFLECT ....

....

....

BINGE-
WATCH A
TV SERIES

with a friend

COMPLETED ON ....

REFLECT ....

....

....

SET UP A WEEKLY MOVIE DATE

with friends

COMPLETED ON ....

REFLECT ....

....

....

TRY A FREE CLASS

at the community college

COMPLETED ON ....

REFLECT ....

....

....

PICK OUT
A PODCAST

for someone else

COMPLETED ON ....

REFLECT ....

....

....

TRY A NEW RESTAURANT

and chat with the waiter

COMPLETED ON ....

REFLECT ....

....

....

SIGN UP FOR A KICKBALL TEAM

COMPLETED ON ....

REFLECT ....

....

....

HOST A
FRIENDSGIVING

COMPLETED ON ....

REFLECT ....

....

....

SHOW UP TO TRIVIA NIGHT

and join a team

COMPLETED ON ....

REFLECT ....

....

....

STOP BY A COWORKER'S DESK

just to say hi

COMPLETED ON ....

REFLECT ....

....

....

CHAT WITH THE SHOPKEEPER

while browsing a store

COMPLETED ON ....

REFLECT ....

....

....

DO SOMEONE A FAVOR

COMPLETED ON ....

REFLECT ....

....

....

HELP
WITHOUT
BEING ASKED

COMPLETED ON ....

REFLECT ....

....

....

SHOP LOCAL

COMPLETED ON ....

REFLECT ....

....

....

WORK OUT
OUTSIDE

COMPLETED ON ....

REFLECT ....

....

....

CHECK OUT A LOCAL TOURIST ATTRACTION

COMPLETED ON ....

REFLECT ....

....

....

CHAT WITH THE BARTENDER

COMPLETED ON ....

REFLECT ....

....

....

SET ASIDE TIME FOR HANGING OUT

COMPLETED ON ....

REFLECT ....

....

....

LEARN A FRIEND'S LOVE LANGUAGE

COMPLETED ON ....

REFLECT ....

....

....

GIVE SOMEONE ADVICE

COMPLETED ON ....

REFLECT ....

....

....

HOLD A BABY

(but ask permission first)

COMPLETED ON ....

REFLECT ....

....

....

PLAY
WITH
A CAT

COMPLETED ON ....

REFLECT ....

....

....

PLAY
TAG

FIND A
RUNNING
CLUB

COMPLETED ON ....

REFLECT ....

....

....

PUT YOURSELF OUT THERE

COMPLETED ON ....

REFLECT ....

....

....

CARPOOL

COMPLETED ON ....

REFLECT ....

....

....

LEND SOMEONE A BOOK

COMPLETED ON ....

REFLECT ....

....

....

OFFER
SUPPORT

COMPLETED ON ....

REFLECT ....

....

....

SHARE A DRINK

COMPLETED ON ....

REFLECT ....

....

....

BUY THE FIRST ROUND

COMPLETED ON ....

REFLECT ....

....

....

WORK
TOGETHER

INVITE YOURSELF OVER

COMPLETED ON ....

REFLECT ....

....

....

HAVE WHAT SHE'S HAVING

COMPLETED ON ....

REFLECT ....

....

....

ORDER FAMILY-STYLE

COMPLETED ON ....

REFLECT ....

....

....

ORGANIZE A HAPPY HOUR AFTER WORK

COMPLETED ON ....

REFLECT ....

....

....

HARMONIZE

LEND A HAND

COMPLETED ON ....

REFLECT ....

....

....

SHARE YOUR SUCCESSES

COMPLETED ON ....

REFLECT ....

....

....

DONATE OLD CLOTHES TO A SHELTER

COMPLETED ON ....

REFLECT ....

....

....

START AN ANNUAL EVENT WITH FRIENDS

COMPLETED ON ....

REFLECT ....

....

....

GIVE A WARM HANDSHAKE

COMPLETED ON ....

REFLECT ....

....

....

FLIRT, JUST A LITTLE

COMPLETED ON ....

REFLECT ....

....

....

MAKE A
SCRAPBOOK

COMPLETED ON ....

REFLECT ....

....

....

PICK UP
THE TAB

COMPLETED ON ....

REFLECT ....

....

....

SAY HI IN THE ELEVATOR

COMPLETED ON ....

REFLECT ....

....

....

ASK SOMEONE AT THE GYM TO SPOT YOU

COMPLETED ON ....

REFLECT ....

....

....

SHARE YOUR FAVORITE SPOT

with a new friend

COMPLETED ON ....

REFLECT ....

....

....

DO SOMETHING UNEXPECTED

for someone else

COMPLETED ON ....

REFLECT ....

....

....

SURPRISE
SOMEONE

COMPLETED ON ....

REFLECT ....

....

....

CONGRATULATE COWORKERS ON THEIR SUCCESSES

COMPLETED ON ....

REFLECT ....

....

....

HELP PEOPLE WHO ARE LOST

COMPLETED ON ....

REFLECT ....

....

....

TELL PEOPLE

that you appreciate them

COMPLETED ON ....

REFLECT ....

....

....

GET TO KNOW PEOPLE

at your local stores

COMPLETED ON ....

REFLECT ....

....

....

CHAT
WITH THE
BUTCHER

COMPLETED ON ....

REFLECT ....

....

....

SAY HI TO THE CROSSING GUARD

COMPLETED ON ....

REFLECT ....

....

....

SNEAK A NOTE IN A FRIEND'S POCKET

COMPLETED ON ....

REFLECT ....

....

....

MAKE SOMEONE LAUGH

COMPLETED ON ....

REFLECT ....

....

....

EXCHANGE
FRIENDSHIP
BRACELETS

COMPLETED ON ....

REFLECT ....

....

....

WAVE AT A TOUR BUS

COMPLETED ON ....

REFLECT ....

....

....

START
LEARNING
A NEW
LANGUAGE

COMPLETED ON ....

REFLECT ....

....

....

MAKE SOMEONE SMILE

COMPLETED ON ....

REFLECT ....

....

....

RETELL FAMILY STORIES

COMPLETED ON ....

REFLECT ....

....

....

WATCH THE CITY LIGHTS

and imagine the people inside

COMPLETED ON ....

REFLECT ....

....

....

SNUGGLE

COMPLETED ON ....

REFLECT ....

....

....

TALK WITH PEOPLE

while waiting in line

COMPLETED ON ....

REFLECT ....

....

....

ADMIT WHEN YOU'RE HAVING A BAD DAY

COMPLETED ON ....

REFLECT ....

....

....

LOOK OUT THE WINDOW

COMPLETED ON ....

REFLECT ....

....

....

ASK YOUR PARENTS FOR STORIES

about their childhood

COMPLETED ON ....

REFLECT ....

....

....

GO TO A REUNION

COMPLETED ON ....

REFLECT ....

....

....

CRASH A PARTY

COMPLETED ON ....

REFLECT ....

....

....

PLAY
A DUET

COMPLETED ON ....

REFLECT ....

....

....

TAKE SILLY PHOTOS WITH A FRIEND

COMPLETED ON ....

REFLECT ....

....

....

TEXT A PHOTO TO YOUR MOM

COMPLETED ON ....

REFLECT ....

....

....

WRITE BACK

COMPLETED ON ....

REFLECT ....

....

....

WRITE A SONG FOR SOMEONE

COMPLETED ON ....

REFLECT ....

....

....

CALL
BACK

COMPLETED ON ....

REFLECT ....

....

....

LEAVE
A SILLY
VOICEMAIL

COMPLETED ON ....

REFLECT ....

....

....

DONATE BOOKS TO YOUR LIBRARY

COMPLETED ON ....

REFLECT ....

....

....

BUILD A LITTLE FREE LIBRARY

COMPLETED ON ....

REFLECT ....

....

....

GIVE MONEY TO A STREET PERFORMER

COMPLETED ON ....

REFLECT ....

....

....

HAVE A
NIGHT IN

with friends

COMPLETED ON ....

REFLECT ....

....

....

DANCE CHEEK TO CHEEK

COMPLETED ON ....

REFLECT ....

....

....

START A PILLOW FIGHT

COMPLETED ON ....

REFLECT ....

....

....

KNIT
SOMETHING

for someone else

COMPLETED ON ....

REFLECT ....

....

....

VENT YOUR FRUSTRATIONS

COMPLETED ON ....

REFLECT ....

....

....

INVITE A FRIEND ON A WALK

COMPLETED ON ....

REFLECT ....

....

....

HAVE LUNCH WITH YOUR COWORKERS

COMPLETED ON ....

REFLECT ....

....

....

SMILE AT A STRANGER

COMPLETED ON ....

REFLECT ....

....

....

LET SOMEONE STAND UNDER YOUR UMBRELLA

COMPLETED ON ....

REFLECT ....

....

....

FORGIVE A FRIEND

COMPLETED ON ....

REFLECT ....

....

....

MAKE A TIME CAPSULE

and imagine who might find it

COMPLETED ON ....

REFLECT ....

....

....

TALK ABOUT YOUR GOALS

LET YOUR EMOTIONS OUT

COMPLETED ON ....

REFLECT ....

....

....

REREAD
OLD
LETTERS

COMPLETED ON ....

REFLECT ....

....

....

TELL PEOPLE WHEN YOU MISS THEM

COMPLETED ON ....

REFLECT ....

....

....

CATCH UP OVER COFFEE

COMPLETED ON ....

REFLECT ....

....

....

PLAY THE LICENSE PLATE GAME

on a long car ride

COMPLETED ON ....

REFLECT ....

....

....

TREAT A FRIEND TO A MEAL

COMPLETED ON ....

REFLECT ....

....

....

BUY DONUTS FOR THE OFFICE

COMPLETED ON ....

REFLECT ....

....

....

HAVE DEEP CONVERSATIONS

COMPLETED ON ....

REFLECT ....

....

....

TEXT
BACK

COMPLETED ON ....

REFLECT ....

....

....

LEAVE A BIG TIP

COMPLETED ON ....

REFLECT ....

....

....

WRITE A SECRET MESSAGE

COMPLETED ON ....

REFLECT ....

....

....

CHEER SOMEONE UP

COMPLETED ON ....

REFLECT ....

....

....

ASK FOR SOMEONE'S OPINION

COMPLETED ON ....

REFLECT ....

....

....

GO ON A SPONTANEOUS DATE

COMPLETED ON ....

REFLECT ....

....

....

HAVE A FRIENDLY DEBATE

COMPLETED ON ....

REFLECT ....

....

....

LOG OFF
A SOCIAL
NETWORK

for a week

COMPLIMENT THE CHEF

COMPLETED ON ....

REFLECT ....

....

....

What else can you do?

COMPLETED ON ....

REFLECT ....

....

....

What else can you do?

COMPLETED ON ....

REFLECT ....

....

....

What else can you do?

COMPLETED ON ....

REFLECT ....

....

....

What else can you do?

COMPLETED ON ....

REFLECT ....

....

....

What else can you do?

COMPLETED ON ....

REFLECT ....

....

....

What else can you do?

COMPLETED ON ....

REFLECT ....

....

....

What else can you do?

COMPLETED ON ....

REFLECT ....

....

....

What else can you do?

COMPLETED ON ....

REFLECT ....

....

....

What else can you do?

What else can you do?

COMPLETED ON ....

REFLECT ....

....

....

What else can you do?